LEAD GEN

Kaizen

改善

How To Generate
More Leads Than Your Business Can Handle
By Implementing Lead Generation Fundamentals
And Avoiding The Major Lead Gen Mistakes

Chaffee-Thanh Nguyen
Key Concept Coaching

Chaffee-Thanh Nguyen

First Printing, 2012
ISBN: 1480053856
ISBN-13: 978-1480053854

DEDICATION

This is dedicated the multitudes of entrepreneurs and small business owners out there working to make a better lives for themselves, their families, and their communities. I offer this book to help you achieve your dreams. Dedication, passion, and persistence will allow you to find your voice and help others find theirs. Celebrate Life!

ACKNOWLEDGMENTS

To my wife, Amy, for putting up with my late nights while testing the concepts in this book. To my son Adam for making me smile every day. To all the students I've coached and worked with for helping me refine the ideas contained within.

CONTENTS

1 CUSTOMERS ARE GOOD FOR BUSINESS

Customers are good for business. I bet you knew that.

In fact, it's pretty common sense. Unfortunately, many businesses actually forget that sometimes. Instead, they focus on products or services which while good in theory, don't always translate into sales.

Take for example Apple Macintosh in the 80's. Apple Macintosh had the far better computer system than Microsoft back then. Yet Apple's insistent focus on their product (which was again the superior product), almost put them out of business. Microsoft instead focused on sales and marketing and getting more customers.

Microsoft went on to become one of the fastest growing companies in the 80's and Apple Macintosh again, almost went out of business. In fact, they were 3 months away from claiming bankruptcy when Steve Jobs came back to the helm of Apple in the late 90's.

In every business, there's always a balance between providing good products and services versus getting sales and running a profitable business. Obviously a business has to have products and services that people like and use - otherwise eventually, not matter how good your marketing and sales are, people will catch on and your company will go out of business.

Do you know what the most profitable skill is for running your business though? As I showed above, it's not having the best product. It's not having the best management, the best logistics or inventory. It's marketing your business and making sales. **The only time you bring in money for your business is when you make a sale.**

You can have the best management team in place, fully stocked shelves, the best product in the market, the best processes and procedures, the best training, the best documentation (I think you get my point) and none of that matters unless you make a sale and bring in money. Without sales, you make no money. Without money, you can't pay your employees. Without money, you can't produce more products. Without money, you won't be in business much longer.

This book is not about specific strategies to market and generate leads though. It's about refining your current sales funnels so that you can generate a steady stream of leads and convert them into sales, customers, and most importantly, revenue. While I can teach you specific lead generation strategies, they are constantly changing and with the information presented here, you can develop leads for ANY product or service you are selling at any time. This information is golden and when used right... will produce you gold!

Remember, customers are good for business. So what are you doing to get more customers? When times are tough and budgets are cut, what are you doing to get more customers? Most businesses think that if they cut the marketing budget, focus on internal cost reductions and restructuring that business will grow.

If your business is bloated, this will all definitely help reduce your operating expenses. It won't however actually increase revenue. No marketing, no lead generation means fewer customers which means less business. Less business means less revenue.

This sounds pretty basic and straight forward right? You would think. Except studies show, that most businesses still don't think that way.

Take a look at this study done by CSO Insights in 2009. Their Sales Performance Optimization Study showed that 97% of CEOs interviewed planned on increasing revenue that year. What's more, the study showed that 67% of CEOs plan in increasing revenue while reducing sales headcount. Remember, fewer sales reps mean fewer people in lead generation. Less lead generation usually translates into fewer sales, and of course, fewer sales usually results in less revenue.

Again, nothing here is rocket science. This is a fundamental understanding of running a business. Fewer customers typically mean fewer sales which typically means less revenue. Less revenue leads to more budget cuts and well, it's a vicious cycle.

If this is so obvious, why do businesses keep on doing the same thing and making the same mistake?

The truth is that most businesses know that lead generation is important and know they need to do it; they just don't really do it or don't understand how to do it properly. Marketing in general is one of the most misunderstood skills on the entire planet. The main reason behind this is that they think that lead generation is difficult, expensive, and extremely time consuming... and if done improperly, they are correct.

I'm sure you've even heard that a prospect must see something 7 times before they take action. Yet why do 95% of sales people quit after the 4th attempt (Many don't even make it to the 4th attempt)?

Getting rejected 6 times before getting accepted can become tiring. It can be discouraging. It can be upsetting. So it's easier to see if you can find a new prospect instead of trudging through until the 7th or even 8th contact. Just because it's easier though doesn't mean it's right.

Let's face it, most business owners don't understand advertising, marketing, and lead generation. What's more, they have a difficult time trusting anyone to help them get started and if they have hired someone to help them, they probably got burned.

They probably spent a lot of money and got very little or no results. So now they're gun-shy. It's easier for them to focus on their product or service - which is something they do know - versus focusing on sales and marketing -which is something they don't know, and sometimes, downright scary to them.

Because of this fear or lack of understanding, they don't do what needs to be done to market and sell their product or service and eventually go out of business.

So welcome to Lead Gen Kaizen. In this book, we're going to focus on Professional Lead Generation Best Practices and the top lead generation mistakes that businesses make (and more importantly, how to avoid them). By following these best practices and avoiding the major lead generation mistakes, you can continually improve your lead generation strategies and get more customers with less effort.

2 UNDERSTANDING THE SALES PROCESS

It is critical that you understand the sales process. Most people think that just because they met someone at a networking event that they should be getting sales. They think that if they post something on Facebook or Twitter that they should be getting sales. Their sales funnel goes from meet someone to sale without anything in between.

And the sad thing is that most people know better. What they actually do though does not reflect what they ultimately know deep down inside. Knowing and doing are two different things and it's easy to just meet someone, expect a sale, and then get disappointed when it doesn't happen. It's not as easy following the full sales process and setting up the proper sales funnels.

While this isn't a course on the Sales Process and Sales Funnels, it's important that you understand this process in order to be successful with lead generation and conversions. So let's do a quick outline of the sales process.

Step 1: Lead Generation

Lead generation is basically getting people to raise their hand and say, "I'm interested. Give me more." It's getting them to take that first action step of asking for more information. It is NOT a sale and does not mean that they will buy from you. This step is simply getting people interested, not completing the sales cycle.

Step 2: Qualifying and Fact Finding

This is a very important step and can be the difference between success and failure. You must qualify your prospect to see if they're even interested or a potential person to purchase from you.

You've got to do some fact finding and ask them questions so they can filter themselves in or out of the next step. If they're not interested, then you shouldn't be spending your precious time trying to convince them into the next step.

There are thousands of interested people out there, so you just have to make it easy for them to find you. If someone's not interested (qualified), then wish them the best of luck and move on to the next prospect. This is where you can really get to know your potential prospect a lot more.

Step 3: Presentation and Rapport Building

Present your products and services to the prospect and sell them on what you've got. Don't just tell them what you've got and overwhelm them with facts and figures.

Sell them what you've got and tell them stories of how people have used and loved your product and service. Share with them testimonials and benefits of how your product or service can make an impact in their life. SELL them on your product, service, company, and brand.

Remember, facts tell, stories sell. Get them to know you and your business and build a rapport with them and sell them on your product or service.

Step 4: Address Objections and Answer Questions

Objections are nothing more than a request for more information. Unless someone comes out with a straight out, "no, I'm not interested", then what they are really saying is, "I need more information before I make a final decision." Answer their questions directly and use stories to drive home concepts and ideas. Give them more information and answer their questions. This gives them a sense of confidence in you and your business while building your expert status.

Step 5: Close The Sale

Unfortunately, many businesses don't remember this step. They have no challenge talking about their product or service, yet they are afraid to ask for the money. Ask for the money. Get the sale. If you don't make the sale, then you don't make any money. So close them and ask for the sale. If you've got a good product or service that you believe in, then you're doing them a favor by selling them something that's going to make their life better. So close the sale.

Step 6: Anchor the Sale

There's a term out there called buyer's remorse. This is where people feel that they made a purchase that they should not have and want a refund. After you close the sale, anchor the sale to something important to that individual and they will never feel buyer's remorse.

For example, if someone wants something for a significant other, don't just sell them on the benefits of the product, anchor them to how the product will make their significant other feel. Anchor them on how grateful their significant other will be and how happy it will make them when they see the product or service. Have them visualize giving the product to their significant other and imagine the reaction they'll receive from them. This anchors and solidifies the sale so that it won't be returned for any reason.

Step 7: Ask for Referrals

There's no better time to get referrals than right after the sale. The customer is in a generous mood and it's best to ask them right there and then for others they'd like to share their good fortune with.

So there you have it... the 7 Step Sales Process. When you keep these steps in mind when developing your sales funnel, your conversions and sales will skyrocket. Too often businesses only focus on one or two of these steps. It's important to have all 7 steps in play at all times in order to have a constant flow of business. So with that, let's move on to the next section of this book which are the fundamental rules of professional lead generation.

3 A STEADY STREAM OF LEADS

Believe it or not, there are literally THOUSANDS of hungry consumers are searching for you. Well, at least for your product or service if not for you. **This is great news because the first fundamental rule of lead generation is that you must have a steady stream of leads coming into your business at all times.**

The mistake that many businesses make is that they run a marketing campaign for a short period of time; get some customers (if they're lucky or doing it right), and then focus on servicing those customers while stopping their lead generation strategies.

Again, while this sounds good in theory, the challenge arises when they're done servicing those customers and then have nothing in the pipeline to work on. Then they have to start over from square one.

If they had a constant stream of leads, they could focus on converting those leads to new customers and have a line of customers ready to work with throughout the year. In order to generate a steady stream of leads, you need to continually run your lead generation strategies.

Just because you get a few customers doesn't mean you should stop your lead generation. There are literally thousands of hungry customers searching for you and you just have to make it easy for them to find you.

Of course this can become time consuming or overwhelming if you're doing everything at once and spending too much time on generating leads and not servicing them, so it's important that you put together your marketing strategy and execute properly. A combination of lead generation and customer delivery and service is very important.

So step 1 for Lead Gen Kaizen is to review your lead generation methods and ensure that you have enough in place to continually provide your business with a stream of leads coming in all the time - even when you're not actively working it.

You need multiple lead generation efforts all running at once. Whether you're advertising on the radio, TV, internet or magazines, you should also have classified ads, an updated website, promotional materials, events, and more. All these campaigns should be running conjointly to produce you an endless supply of leads.

We'll talk about how you can accomplish this later on in the book and for now; let's move on to the second fundamental rule of professional lead generation.

4 NO IMPULSE BUYS

Have you ever been shopping at the department store and saw something and just had to have it? A few bucks later and you're going home a happy camper. That's what we call an impulse buy.

Impulse buys are great for the person selling the product or service! We all want impulse buyers. **Unfortunately, most prospective clients do not make "impulse" buys.**

I can't tell you how many times I've heard people tell me that they sent out a tweet, made a post on Facebook, or created a flyer and passed it out to people and they didn't get a single sale. Then they get all upset and tell me that lead generation on Facebook, Twitter, or social media doesn't work.

Listen, most people don't make impulse buys when it comes to things they need or high priced items.

I had a co-worker who once spent 6 months of in-depth research on different cars before he actually went out and bought one. He just didn't see a flyer and then go to a dealer and buy a car. He spent weeks on end researching different features, benefits, and designs.

Once he felt comfortable that he was getting everything he wanted, he made the purchase. When you can educate your prospect and get them comfortable, then they're going to be more likely to purchase something.

The truth is that as much as you (or your sales team) might like to shorten the sales cycle, buying complex, important, trust-based products and services takes time.

Don't listen to some fly-by-night operation that tells you that only one mailing to 15,000 homes is going to give you great results. Most businesses that I've worked with have gotten very little to NO results for just a quick mailing.

As I've said before, most people don't make impulse buys and they need to see things multiple times before making a purchase - remember that IBM study about seeing things 7 times?

A strategic marketing plan with multiple ways for a prospect to see your message is critical to your success. Focus on developing sales funnels and marketing campaigns, not just a blast here or there. When you can design a sales funnel a multi-pronged and multiple touch strategy and execute, you'll start getting sales. When you try to take shortcuts, you just wasted a lot of time with no results.

So don't focus too much on the quick, one-time, impulse buyer. Focus instead on developing automated sales funnels designed to build a relationship with your prospect and entice them to buy when they're ready to buy.

5 HOW NOW PURPLE COW

In his book, <u>Purple Cow: Transform Your Business by Being Remarkable</u>, noted author Seth Godin talks about how he was driving through France and saw, "hundreds of storybook cows grazing in lovely pastures right next to the road."

At first he marveled at their beauty. Then after a while, he just started ignoring them. Every new cow he passed looked just like the prior one and they were all starting to get boring. As he says, "what was once amazing was now common." If you've seen enough of them, you'd call them boring as well. They may be magnificent, well-bred animals, and after enough of them, they'd still get boring.

So what about a Purple Cow? A purple cow amongst a throng of regular ordinary brown cows - now that would be outstanding. It would be truly remarkable and worth talking about. The brown cows however, quickly became invisible.

While there are many remarkable things in this world, it's also filled with a bunch of boring stuff. This holds true for lead generation as well.

Most lead generation strategies are well... boring. As Seth says, "Remarkable marketing is the art of building things worth noticing right into your product or service. Not just slapping on the marketing function as a last-minute add-on, but also understanding from the outset that if your offering itself isn't remarkable, then it's invisible -- no matter how much you spend on well-crafted advertising."

So the next rule of Powerful, Professional Lead Generation is that you must create a compelling offer to attract leads.

We all know the saying, "Give and you shall receive." That's true in the world of business as well. Your offer, product, or service must be compelling enough that someone is going to take that first step to contact you, return your call, or even purchase your product or service. What are you offering your clients and is it compelling enough to get them to take action.

Marketing 101 covers the concept of **A-I-D-A or Attention-Interest-Desire-Action**. Notice that the first step is attention. What are you offering and is it going to grab the attention of someone?

That's why outrageous marketing works sometimes.

Take a look at PETA.

PETA uses ads with naked celebrities. While you may or may not support PETA, their ads grab a viewer's attention. Once you grab their attention, then you must peak their interest, stir up a desire, and motivate them to take action. None of that matters though if you don't grab their attention first.

Here's a sample Peta.org press release:

> **Fresno, Calif. --** Wearing nothing but strategically placed lettuce leaves and holding signs that read, "Go Green, Go Vegan," a pair of PETA "Lettuce Ladies" will hand out free vegan food in Fresno on Friday. After filling up their stomachs, the first 20 customers to line up at the pumps will also receive two free gallons of gas, which will be pumped by a lovely Lettuce Lady.
>
> *Source: http://www.peta.org/mediacenter/news-releases/PETA-s-Sexy--Lettuce--Ladies--Fight-Prices-at-the-Pump-by-Giving-Away-Gasoline-in-Fresno.aspx

Think that women wearing nothing but strategically placed lettuce leaves would catch someone's eye. If that doesn't do it, maybe the free food and free gas for the first 20 people will. Notice, not only are they using outrageous marketing, they're making an outrageous offer of free food and free gas. Since gas today costs about an arm and a leg, that's quite tempting for some people.

So remember this rule of professional lead generation. Create a compelling offer which will grab a prospect's attention.

What's your purple cow? What's your compelling offer? If it doesn't make you want to jump at it, chances are others won't want to jump either. Make your offer jump and watch your conversions into sales and customers jump as well!

6 YOU'VE BEEN MEASURED

I know that you're probably not a carpenter, so who cares about this measuring stuff right?

Wrong.

You should care. You should definitely care.

The next rule of Professional Lead Generation is often overlooked even though it may be one of the most important steps. This rule is to simply **measure, test, and improve your lead generation and nurturing efforts on an ongoing basis.**

This is what Lead Gen Kaizen is all about. Kaizen stands for continuous improvement. You're always making continuous improvement to your lead generation efforts. Measuring and testing your lead generation efforts will allow you to see what's working and what's not working. This of course will save you time, money, and energy.

I can't tell you how many businesses I've run across that will spend thousands of dollars on a mailing campaign and have no clue how effective that campaign was for them. Think about it. If you're doing a complete mailing campaign that would be composed of between 5 - 8 letters and postcards (because we know that just one mailing is not enough).

Let's just use 5 mailings (3 letters and 2 post cards) for easy math. A typical mailing campaign would cover about 1000 households (I've seen some cover up to 5,000 - 10,000 mailings and some less depending upon how targeted the mailing list is).

A letter costs $0.45 to mail today. Throw in the cost of the paper for the letter, the envelop, and the labor to create and mail it and you're at about $0.75 a letter or more. A postcard will run about $0.65.

So let's do the math.

$0.75 times 1000 letters is $750.00.
$750.00 times 3 letters is $2,250.00.
$0.65 times 1000 postcards is $650.00.
$650.00 times 2 postcards is $1,300.00.

So the total cost of a 5 series mailing campaign to 1000 households is $2,250.00 + $1,300.00 = $3,550.00.

Now if you just spent $3,550.00, wouldn't you want to know if that worked or not? Unfortunately, a lot of businesses don't know the results and they're "sold" on doing it again and spending that much money again.

That was a somewhat complicated example, so let's take a look at an easier example. I know a business that spends $800 on a newspaper ad every month in the local paper. They're in a contract for 6 months.

That's' $4,800. I asked them if it was working for them and they said, "I think so." I asked them if they got any customers from the ad and they said, "I don't know for sure. I never really asked."

Now because they "think" that it worked, when the six months is up, chances are, they are going to renew their newspaper ad. If they were selling a $500 widget and the ad worked because they were able to sell 1 widget a month from the ad, they'll realize that they only made $3,000. Sure the ad worked and if you did the math, they spent $4,800 to make $3,000. Anyone can see that is a losing proposition.

Even if you're working on a simple flyer campaign, every flyer should be tracked. A simple trick to track different marketing campaigns is have people call in and mention a special code. It could be any code you make up and if you're passing out 4 different flyers, you can have 4 different codes. Track the number of codes that come in and you can tell which flyer is the most effective or which area of distribution is the most effective.

Whatever your lead generation method is, it is extremely important that you track it, measure it, test it, and most importantly, improve it or get rid of it if it isn't working.

7 IBRAND, UBRAND, WE ALL BRAND

Branding is an important part of any business. Unfortunately, like Professional Lead Generation, most businesses have no clue how to really brand, do it wrong or do too little of it.

Fortunately, when you do lead generation properly, you can kill two birds with one stone! Why is that? Because one of the fundamental rules of lead generation is to build your brand through lead generation efforts.

That's right. **You can and should be building your brand with every lead generation effort out there.**

There's a saying out there that says, "all things being equal, people will do business with people they know, like, and trust." I'm sure you've heard that before. And while it's true most of the time, most people forget that "all things being NOT equal, people will do business with people they know, like, and trust."

Yup.

People will pay more or put up with more in order to work with someone they know, like, and trust, even if someone out there is less expensive, more reliable, or better qualified.

That's why building a solid brand and a good reputation is so important, and using the proper lead generation strategies is an important part of building a brand.

Before I go further here though, let's just clarify what branding is or is not. Branding is NOT a logo. While having a cool logo is part of a complete brand image, a logo in and of itself is not a brand. Branding is not a company. While knowing what a particular company means you have an idea of what the brand is, the company itself is not a brand. What about a product or service?

Nope. That's not a brand either.

Let's look, for example, at the company that does branding probably better than any other company out there... Apple.

When you look at the Apple logo of well... and Apple, what comes to mind? When you think of Apple the company, what comes to mind? How about the iPhone 5 or the iPad. What do you think about when you think about Steve Jobs? Is Steve Jobs the Apple brand?

When you think of Apple overall, how do you feel? And there it is... how does it make you feel? You see, a brand is a feeling. It's an emotional response to a company, product, logo, or service. It's a lifestyle.

Even if you've never used an Apple product before, there's a level of quality and comfort that you just expect from it. Of course their product must work as advertised or better and if you examine their lead generation efforts (yes, even Apple works on generating new leads) every piece of marketing they have brands their company and adds to the Apple lifestyle.

When you think of Apple, you think of quality, ease of use, design superiority - and that's all before you even use the actual product itself.

A brand is something that creates an emotional response in its customers, prospects, members, and employees. It's not the actual company, logo, or product. It's the response you get when you think about those things.

Whenever you send out a mailing, create a flyer, give someone your business card, those are all lead generation strategies. Each one of those items should contain a consistent brand message which creates an overall feeling of trust for your products or services.

Part of the marketing process and lead generation is building your company brand. Unfortunately, most companies don't even think about this when they work on lead generation. They might think about putting out a great offer or a coupon or some kind of incentive. Their focus though is the incentive, offer, or discount, not branding their business.

When you think about every message you put out there and if that message is congruent with your brand, then every lead generation channel is an opportunity to add to your reputation. One small change or tweak can generate huge results.

8 LOVE IT!

Bill Gates once said, "The first rule of any technology used in a business is that automation applied to an efficient operation will magnify the efficiency."

When using Lead Generation properly, the goal is to automate, automate, and automate! The more you can automate your lead generation methods, the more you can focus on what you're really good at or what you really enjoy doing.

Let's face it; most people don't enjoy the lead generation process. If your business is fixing glass and windows, chances are you're good at fixing windows and glass, not selling people on fixing windows and glass.

Like most small businesses, they start because they see a need in the market and they enjoy fulfilling that need, so they start a business so they can do what they enjoy doing. They don't really enjoy selling or marketing or generating leads. They enjoy doing whatever it is that they are doing.

Mechanics enjoy working on cars, not finding people who need their cars worked on. Dentists enjoy fixing teeth, not finding people who need their teeth fixed. A hairstylist enjoys styling hair, not finding people who want their hair styled.

I think you get the point.

Let me drive this point home for a second.

Quickly pull out a sheet of paper.

Draw a line down the middle of the sheet.

On the left side, write down the top 3 things you spend the most time on within your business. Go ahead. Jot it down.

Now on the right side, write down the top 3 things that you WANT to spend the most time on within your business.

Do they match?

Things I Spend the Most Time On	Things I WANT to Spend The Most Time On
1.	1.
2.	2.
3.	3.

Why or why not?

Most people start their own business because they want to work on something they enjoy doing. What happens though is that they start working on the business of business. They lose focus of what's important and what they want to achieve with their business.

The more you can automate your business and lead generation activities, the more you can then focus on what you love to do. What can you do to automate your lead generation efforts?

Here are some tips:

1) Develop sales funnels which automatically market for you. For example, using the internet to create squeeze pages, opt-ins, and auto responder messages which will continually market to your leads.

2) Create online training tutorials and modules using simple PowerPoint presentations and YouTube videos. Instead of spending hours on end training new associates, have them go through the online training modules.

3) Hire someone to care of everything for you. Unfortunately, not every business can afford to hire the right lead generation specialists. Put in another way, good sales people are hard to find. Good commission-only sales people are even more difficult to find.

4) Have a good website which markets and sells your business for you 24 hours a day, 7 days a week. A good website will get picked up by the search engines and when someone does a search for a product or service; your site may show up. Research shows that over 80% of people never go beyond the first page of a search engine results page, so make sure you have a good website and that it's search engine optimized.

5) Create documented sales funnels which walks through step-by-step everything that needs to happen in order to sell a product or service. Use this documentation to train sales associates.

This last one is extremely important just for the functioning of your business. One of my mentors was a multi-millionaire in his early 30's. At the ripe old age of 34, he had an aneurism. Fortunately, he survived only he was hospitalized for 6 months with short term memory loss. He couldn't remember anything 5 minutes out.

As his entire business was in his head, you can see this caused some challenges with his clients and support staff. Since he was hospitalized, he didn't communicate with his clients. His client database was password protected, so no one could access it to let his clients know what had happened. Since there was no communication, some of his paying clients got mad and started sending him no-so-nice messages.

Unfortunately, no one could do anything because all his processes, procedures, products, and services were all undocumented and locked behind passwords.

Fortunately, after 6 months, he started regaining his memory and is now able to conduct business normally, and it was an ugly picture for a while there.

He was only 34 years old, so no one – including himself – ever thought anything would happen to him of this magnitude. Lesson learned though, he now documents everything and h as all his passwords stored in a safety deposit box in case something happens to him again. In addition, he uses his new documentation to automatically on-board and train new associates and support staff – something he did manually himself before. He now automates as much as he can so that he's never going to be a bottleneck again in his business – and he discovered that he now works much less on the mundane business tasks which he didn't enjoy and spends more time developing products and helping people – which he loves to do.

You too can start doing more of what you love. It just takes a little upfront effort to make it happen. Automate, automate, automate and you'll start freeing up your time. Take a close look at your business and see what you can automate then work on making it happen!

9 PROFESSIONAL LEAD GENERATION MISTAKES

Does any of this sound familiar to you:

1)   You've bought thousands of dollars worth of courses and education and you're still not doing something right. You're still not making money or you're still struggling to succeed.

2)   Your business is up and running and making money only it seems like you just can't get ahead. You're working day by day and you need more leads, more prospects, more customers, and more sales!

3)   You've got no clue what you're doing.

Hey if any of these sounds like you or someone you know, then don't worry. You're not alone. Many multi-million dollar businesses are making the same mistakes that the little guys are making.

In fact, many of them are making some very amateurish mistakes that are costing hundreds or thousands if not more. And while some people say that experience is the best teacher, that's really only half right. Someone else's experience is actually the best teacher because they already made the mistakes and you can avoid them and attain a higher level of success much faster!

So in this next section, we will discuss the major mistakes businesses make when it comes to Professional Lead Generation and how you can avoid them and achieve your own successes. In our discussion about professional lead generation fundamentals, we already talked about some of the mistakes people make as they go hand-in-hand. And in this section, we'll take a deeper dive into those mistakes and help you avoid them and achieve success.

10 ME, MYSELF, AND I OR WE, US, AND OUR

The first major mistake is not focusing on the customer.

If you're focused on yourself and what you do, you're not focused on the prospect and what they need. If it's all about you, then it's not about them. If it's not about them, then they won't buy anything. If all someone does is talk about them, how long will you want to talk to them?

In addition, what kind of picture do you get in your head when all you hear someone talk about is themselves? So why would you do that with your business and marketing materials?

Look at your website and your marketing materials and count the I's and we's. Compare that to the you's and your's. If you've got more I's and We's, you've got a copywriting challenge. Change your focus to your client and watch your conversions increase.

In addition, personalize your marketing materials and focus on the prospect whenever possible. Instead of just saying something like, "Increase business by 100% when using XYZ widget", personalize it with the word YOU or YOUR and say instead, "Increase YOUR business by 100% when YOU use XYZ widget."

By doing so, I'm speaking directly to that business owner. This makes them feel special that I spent the time to personalize the message to them (even if I really didn't). Most businesses get generic, canned marketing pieces, so when they get something calling them out specifically, they'll be more likely to go to the next step.

Remember the radio station WII FM. It stands for What's In It For Me? That's the question that is running through a prospects mind when they read or see your marketing materials. People want to know what they're going to get from it.

I remember going to a networking event once and I met a nice guy and asked him what he did. For the next 10 minutes all he did was talk about himself. I don't think I said more than 10 words like uh huh, sure, cool, right. I also nodded my head a few times. When we were done with the conversation, he said that it was the best conversation he's ever had with anyone in a long time and that he felt great. He knew absolutely nothing about me, and that didn't matter because I made him feel good, and he would remember how I made him feel.

Bottom line is that people like to talk about themselves; they like to hear about themselves; they like other people to talk about them, and it makes them feel good. And when they feel good, they are more likely to buy. Focus on your customer and not yourself, your product, or your business and you'll get more conversions.

11 GOING ALL IN

When it comes to marketing and lead generation, most businesses unwittingly go all in. This means that they usually only have one marketing and lead generation method going at once. Sometimes it's a direct mail campaign. Or it may be a six month newspaper advertising campaign. Or it may even be a TV or radio ad. When that campaign is over, then they go on to the next one.

This is really one of the biggest lead generation mistakes you can make - only running one lead generation strategy at a time. To successfully build a lead generation machine, you need to have multiple lead generation channels all working at the same time for you. This really helps get more exposure for your business and it may even be the one thing you need to give your business a boost.

MarketingSherpa research data indicates that trade show speeches, print magazines and online magazines are the top three marketing factors -- aside from word of mouth -- that truly influence more than a third of business purchasing decisions. All three methods are great ways of generating leads. Don't just do one at a time though.

Being a speaker on a podium sometimes create instant expert status and entices people to come talk to you as well. So if you can become a speaker on a stage, then make sure you take that opportunity.

And while having multiple lead generation methods going at once is important; just make sure you're selective in your marketing investments. It doesn't make sense to spend $10,000 on a trade show and then not follow up with any of the leads you get. Make sure you invest in the right things.

I had one client consistently spend $10,000 on trade show booths in different states. Including his time, booth and show materials, and travel expenses, it all added up. I asked him how much business he had gotten from them. He said none yet except he had a few good leads.

Now mind you that he had already spent about a good $50,000 on trade shows at this point. And no, he wasn't doing any other kind of advertising. And no, he didn't have any kind of lead generation and tracking mechanism at his trade show booth. In other words, he would go there, pass out brochures and information, and then just collect the business cards of some potential prospects.

He didn't have a sign-in sheet. He didn't have a sheet where people could request more information. He had no way of tracking how many people actually came to his booth (he did get a list of attendees from the show – which he rarely followed up with). But you know what? He had a good time and felt that he was making progress.

Listen, if I had $50,000 to blow, I'd go on a nice trip with my family for 2 weeks somewhere and live it up instead of going trade shows working my behind off. I would have gotten the same result which is I would have felt better. At least my way I'm not fooling myself into believing I'm actually doing business.

The worst part of it is that he's still going to trade shows with little to no success. Unfortunately, you can only lead a horse to water. He's got to drink it himself.

Remember that you need to have multiple sales funnels working for you all the time in order to have a constant flow of leads and potential customers. Without it, you'll run dry and have to start from square one every time you want a new iclient.

12 YOU'RE A SNOWFLAKE

In addition to going all in with their marketing, another big mistake companies make is funneling all their leads into one big list.

No two snowflakes are alike. People are much the same way. That is, they're different. Depending on where your lead came from, they probably want different things. If you just have a monthly newsletter and you send everyone to that monthly news letter, chances are you're missing out on some opportunities. In addition, some of those people will leave your list.

It's important to segment your list into different funnels of opportunity and meet the needs of each funnel. Segmenting your list (or breaking out your list into different categories) allows you to test out different marketing campaigns to different people and see what works best. It allows you to see which demographic is responding better and allows you to focus your marketing efforts in the right place.

In the case of marketing and lead generation, one size does not fit all. Remember that everyone is different and treating them appropriately will make huge leaps in your sales conversions.

13 FACEBOOK, TWITTER, LINKEDIN... OH MY!

Facebook has over 1 Billion users. You gotta start using it.
Twitter has over 250 million users. You gotta get on it.
LinkedIn is used by all people in all 500 of the Fortune 500
   companies. You gotta jump on it.
Google Plus is the next up and coming social network... you
   gotta get on it.

Any of this sounds familiar to you?

The fact of the matter is that it's easy to get caught up in these social networks only you'll just be spinning your wheels tweeting and posting with no results if you don't have a marketing strategy in place.

As the saying goes, "fail to plan and plan to fail."

Not having a strategic lead generation and marketing plan will cause you to have a lack of focus. Without a point of reference or some marketing goals, you won't know where to go or what to do. Instead you'll just do what feels right at the spur of the moment - which may not always be the best thing to do.

I've been teaching social media lead generation strategies for years now. It always amazing me how little people understand how to use social networks for business. While I don't want to get into an in-depth discussion on different social media strategies (that's an entirely different book), I do want to remind you of one thing. Social networks are just that – social.

People who TRY to sell directly on social networks without first building a relationship with others are just asking for trouble. A Facebook or Twitter account that does nothing except talk about business, their products, and services and then tries to sell something will get absolutely no to extremely low results.

Used properly, social networks are a HUGE source of leads and should be an integral part of anyone's lead generation strategy. If you don't know what you're doing though, then go get some help and/or training. Spend some time online and figure out what you need to do first before you alienate all your friends and fans.

In addition, understanding exactly who your customers are, what your brand message is, and the size of your lead generation budget is critical to your success. It will allow you to focus only on those things which will generate you revenue and bring into light potential opportunities you would otherwise look over. So using social networks goes both ways. It allows the consumer to get to know you and it allows you to get to know and focus on your consumers. Once you have all this information, then you can formulate the proper strategic plan for your lead generation efforts.

Without a strategic lead generation plan, there's a good chance you'll make some expensive mistakes. By having the plan, it lays out guidelines on what you should and should not be investing in and working on. This helps avoids the "Shiny Penny" syndrome where you're just doing the next "cool" thing instead of focusing on your core and strategic initiatives.

Avoid the mistake of acting first without thinking or planning. Put together an effective strategy based upon your business, budget, goals, and existing resources and assets. Define your objective and determine how you're going to measure results. Having the proper marketing strategy in place will ensure you're working on the right things at the right time instead of just spinning your wheels.

14 HOT DATE TONIGHT

Would you ever go up to someone you never met and ask them to marry you? Well, maybe you would, but would they ever say yes? Most likely, any sane person would say no. Why? Because they don't know you. And people like to work with people they know, like, and trust.

So how do you get them to know you?

Well it's kind of like dating. Lead generation that is. First you have to get a prospect to be curious about you and what you're offering. You do this by giving them an offer.

And if they like your offer enough, then they'll stick around to see what else you've got. If they really like what you're offering, then just maybe you got yourself a hot date! If you continue to keep them interested, they'll eventually take the next step and you know... buy something from you of course. What'd you think I was going to say?

Like I said, lead generation is kinda like dating. If the offer is good enough, you'll get a second date. Then a third, etc. etc. and who knows where it will lead. If the offer isn't good enough... well, as they say, there are a lot of fish in the ocean and you'll probably have to go fishing.

Research shows that maybe 1% or 2% of companies running ads use offers to drive readers to their Website. The remaining 98% send people to their home page and effectively eliminating any chance of measuring the ad campaign let alone helping people take that next step.

Hey, that's good news for you because you're going to start giving people offers now if you haven't before. In addition, you should have multiple different offers for different sales funnels.

You can offer white papers, e-courses, special reports, software trials, 30 day trials, and more. The important thing is you offer something of value which will keep the prospect coming back for more until they're ready to become a customer.

The more compelling your offer, the more likely the client will look at it. The headline of your offer is probably one of the most important pieces of the offer.

Take a look at these two headlines:
1) Top 5 Ways To Make Money Online
2) 5 Ways To Explode Your Bank Account Using Simple And Easy To Use Methods A 12 Year Old Can Implement

Which headline do you think would convert more? The second one of course. I've seen people offer things like a free analysis or consultation. For the most part, these things kinds of offers never work. Why? Because just offering a free analysis or consultation doesn't really tell the consumer what they're going to get and how they're going to benefit from it. Sure, it may be implied that they'll get something and they want to hear it. Remember, WII FM?

Even if you say it's worth $395, and say, "Call now for your free consultation", it's not enough. No where in there did it explain the benefits of the analysis and what the analysis might uncover which would be detrimental to the business if it's not taken care of or fixed. No where does it say how the analysis is going to help the business achieve something more. And no where does it convey a sense of urgency where they have to call you right away or else…. The business or prospect simply does not see the benefit of the offer.

If you're going to offer something, then make sure it's a mind-blowing offer which is going to catch someone's attention and tap into an emotional response which will provoke them to into take the action step to call or contact you.

When putting together offers, make sure you don't focus on the product or service you're offering. Your focus needs to be on the benefits to the prospect and what they're going to get by taking the action steps necessary to even get a free offer.

And remember, we're an immediate gratification society. Meaning people want immediate gratification. They don't want an offer that's going to help them 10 years from now. They want an offer that's going to help them today – yesterday!

Your offer has to create a sense of urgency. It's got to trigger an emotional response that says, "if I don't get this NOW I'm going to miss out on something!" Limited quantities, limited time, limited something. People need to act now or they won't get it.

The best place hands down to learn about how to craft good offers is by watching infomercials. Seriously. The marketing geniuses behind infomercials have spent millions if not billions of dollars on researching human behavior and have it down to a science. They use all the marketing strategies they can within a 30 minute period to get people to buy – and it works.

As funny as it may sound, watch and study infomercials (just be careful about buying everything). The more you study them, the better you'll be able to craft your own offers which will entice people to pick up the phone and call you for your product or service.

15 GET A LITTLE TESTY

Do you know what happens when someone goes to your website, tries to contact you and they can't find your contact information or the link to send you a message is broken?

Most of the time they'll leave and never come back meaning you could lose a potential client.

If you set up a landing page and the opt-in doesn't work, guess what may happen?

You could lose a potential client.

If your headline stinks, your conversion ratio may be low. Sometimes something as little as changing one word will double conversion rates.

Broken links, misdirected pages, misspellings... these can all be avoided by testing and re-testing - something most business owners don't do nearly enough. This is a huge mistake!

You want to make sure you thoroughly test your website, marketing materials, lead generation strategies, product brochures, business cards and much, much more. <u>And then test it again!</u> And then keep on testing. With today's rate of change in technology and people's motivations, it's important that you continually test to see what's working best.

In addition, don't just test your website, squeeze page, and opt-in. Make sure you test your email marketing campaigns, your open rates, your headlines, your marketing ads and everything else. The more you test and track results, the more you're going to know what's working and what's not working. Keep testing and tweaking everything and gradually you'll see a huge jump in results.

Make sure you get things right and get it right the first time. As the carpenter says, "measure twice and cut once."

Don't be afraid to use some free tools to help you out either. Google has free Web Optimizer tools. Yield Software has a free testing tool to test landing pages on the fly across three search engines. And while Microsoft Word is not free, using a text editing program with a spell check feature like Microsoft Word for your blog posts and website pages is crucial. I typically type up my blog posts offline in Microsoft Word and then copy and paste it into my blog for posting. It saves me the hassle of losing my internet connection; it has auto save; and it does spell check for me. It's a win all around.

Spending a little time testing can save you a lot of frustration as well as a few potential clients.

16 GOBBLYGOOK

Exactly. What's that.

That's what some businesses have on their webpages and marketing materials.

Gobblygook.

This is simply jargon or words which don't mean anything to anyone except the person who wrote it.

I once read a website that used acronyms all over the place. Unfortunately, they never defined what the acronyms meant. In essence, they were talking a foreign language. So foreign, I left the site without pursuing it any further.

Your potential clients will also do this to your website. **Avoid this big mistake by telling a story instead.** Don't write like a tech geek. Write like a children's book author. Keep it simple and engaging, yet always focused on a point. Avoid the gobblygook and watch your conversions go up.

17 HIGH EXPECTATIONS

Writing one press release won't get you a flood of customers overnight. Just like tweeting once a week won't get you new business contacts every day.

People think that just because they're on Facebook and they became "friends" with someone that they'll suddenly get business. What people forget most of the time that many social networks are just that - social.

I can't tell you how many times I've talked to people who tell me they're on Facebook and Twitter and aren't making any sales. When I ask them what they're doing they tell me they're promoting their business on it. If this is all you're doing, then yes, you'll turn off your potential clients and you won't get any sales.

You can't expect to connect with people online and then expect them to buy something before they even get to know you or your business. You have to nurture that relationship before anyone buys anything. Just because it's online doesn't mean that it's any different than what you have to do offline.

Remember, business is about building relationships, not just selling the heck out of everything. **Don't make the mistake of expecting too much from your marketing campaigns.**

Especially big marketing campaigns. Take SEO or Search Engine Optimization for example. The news out there is that if you're on page 1 of Google then you're going to get a ton of new clients. That's simply not true.

First, it takes working with the right people doing the right things to get your page or website ranked on the first page of Google. Sometimes, depending upon the competition for the keywords you want to get ranked, this can take months or more.

Once you're there, then you will get more visibility and probably more people going to your website. If you don't have the right website set-up with an outrageous purple cow offer so that people will opt-in to a list or call you though, then it was all for naught. Remember that lead generation and sales is a process. Just getting them to your website is the first step of the process. Getting them to take some kind of action where you can capture their information is the second step. Then you have to quantify and qualify them; build a relationship with them; and then get them to buy.

Take things slowly. Start focusing on building real relationships and don't expect sales overnight. Slow and steady wins the race and with a good strategic lead generation strategy, you will get results.

18 WASTING TIME

Imagine if you got $86,400 in the bank every day. The stipulation is that you must spend all of it that day or you lose it. The following day you'll get another $86,400 which you've got to spend-it or lose-it. And you never know when it will stop coming, so you can't just assume it'll be there the next day. Would you spend it? If you got that much ever day would you spend it all every day?

Well that's what's happening every day. Everybody gets 86,400 seconds a day to spend as we please. And when the day's over, so are the seconds. Every day you get another 86,400 seconds only you never know when it's going to end (remember my 34 year old mentor? He got lucky. Another one of my mentors died at age 31 while taking a race car course. He got into an accident and died).

How much time are you spending on your marketing and lead generation methods? More importantly, is it working?

Are you bringing in more money than you are spending? Are you even tracking how much it's costing you? Unfortunately, most businesses don't track their activities and continue working on things that don't produce ROI. This not only costs money, it costs time and energy.

Albert Einstein once said that the definition of insanity is, "doing the same thing over and over and expecting different results." That's why a lot of business owners are insane. They make the same mistake and do the same thing over and over, thinking that they'll get different results.

If you're marketing and lead generation efforts don't work, then stop doing it. Do something else. Keep testing, measuring, tweaking, and then do more testing until you get something that works. And then keep on testing and tweaking. Something that makes you a 10% ROI might be working and with a few tweaks, it might get you a 20% ROI or more. Remember the mistake about not testing enough?

When you find something that works, spend more time doing it and less time doing the things that don't work. Focus on what works and you'll see your results sky rocket.

19 IN THE RED ZONE

Does your company or business have a lot of red tape?

Red tape was first used by Charles V of the 16th century Spanish administration to separate the important dossiers or documents from the normal ones. It has since become known as excessive regulation or rigid conformity to formal rules that is considered redundant or bureaucratic and hinders or prevents action or decision-making and is most closely identified with our current congress and judicial system.

It's also closely identified with companies and businesses which can't seem to get anything done either. Marketing is often based upon current events and trends. If there's too much indecision when implementing a marketing campaign the trend could be over and the opportunity for generating lots of leads could be over.

Many companies make the mistake of having too much red tape and not making decisions fast enough to actually count. It's important that your marketing and lead generation efforts stay current and has the flexibility to make the appropriate decisions when necessary.

Case in point... I saw a tweet the other day advertising as sale for someone's product. It said, "Make sure you enter the sweepstakes and win big!" and then it listed a website link.

When you click on that link the sweepstakes ended over a month ago. Yet for some reason, the tweet was still being sent out. This leaves an impression that the company (or at least the sales rep) is incompetent or at least not paying attention to their own business. It of course turns me off from wanting to do business with them and that's just from a simple tweet.

Imagine if it was an entire marketing campaign instead of just a single tweet!

Why didn't they stop this tweet from going out? Who knows. Could be a number of reasons. And it didn't leave a good impression one way or another. At least though this was in the tail end of the campaign. Imagine if you wanted to do a Christmas campaign and couldn't get it approved until the new year. Guess you just missed that boat.

Imagine if a newspaper reporter had to go through a bunch of red tape to get the morning news reported. Oftentimes something happens and you hear about it in the news the next day. What if something happened and it took the newspaper 2 weeks to get their articles and stories approved. How long with that newspaper last before people stopped reading "old news" and stopped buying it.

Make sure you don't have red tape holding you up from doing or undoing what needs to happen for your business and lead generation efforts.

20 FEEL THE TURTLE, BE THE TURTLE

I was working with a real estate investor who sends out postcards to different neighborhoods. He's been sending these postcards out for years. He tells me that every now and then he'll get a deal from a postcard he sent out over 3 years earlier.

If he would have just done a 1, 2, or even 3 month campaign, he would not still be getting deals from 3 years prior. He's an example of running a lead generation campaign for the long term.

Most companies sign up for newspaper ads, magazine ads, tv, radio, and more for a period of 3 – 6 months and then stop. Depending upon your budget and timeframe, if it's not getting you any kind of ROI, then that's understandable. And whenever you go into a marketing campaign, plan for the long-term. As we learned as kids, the slow turtle wins the race over the fast rabbit. Feel the turtle; Be the turtle.

A consistent, long-term campaign has the added benefit of building your business brand. While someone may not be ready to buy your product or service, if they see your marketing materials over and over again months on end (and even years), then when they are ready, they have a greater chance of contacting you than someone else they just saw in one short commercial. Just being present all the time and building a reputation of stability increases your win factor.

21 BUTTERFINGERS

IBM did a study years ago (which still holds true) which shows that a prospect must see something 7 times before they take action. Yet most sales people quit after only 4 attempts.

Dropping leads (butterfingers...) and not nurturing leads is a huge mistake when it comes to lead generation and conversion into customers.

It's been a common theme throughout this book that sales is a process and that it takes time to build relationships. While it may seem easier to move onto the next lead, if the first lead never said no, then what they're saying is, "I need more information."

People like to feel like they are educated and well informed before they make a buying decision. When you educate leads and nurture them by providing them additional information, benefits, specials, then you're going to be more likely to convert them into a client. If all you do is say, "buy from me" or "buy, buy, buy", then you're going to turn them off and they'll go elsewhere.

If they never hear from you again after the first or second contact, then they'll go somewhere else as well. Remember the term, "out of sight out of mind."

You must nurture leads and continually educate them on the benefits of your product or service. This also continues to brand your business and when they are ready to do business, they'll do it with you.

Remember, people like to do business with people they know, like, and trust. Getting to know, like, and trust you and your business takes time. When you automate your lead generation and sales funnels, you can build relationships on autopilot and when someone is ready for your product or service, guess who they're going to call?

22 THE BEST BANG FOR THE BUCK

Most marketing and lead generation focuses on specials or discounts. Get a $20 discount when you buy now. Hey, $20 may sound like a great deal unless the product is a $2,000 product or more. Then maybe $20 ain't so hot.

Even if you market a percentage like 10%, those are just numbers. While you'll hit a small percentage of the market who are accountants and engineers, when all you do is talk numbers, you're tuning out most of the population.

When developing your lead generation strategies and marketing techniques, keep in mind that facts tell and stories tell. Communicate the value that the client will receive when they use your product or service.

Focus on telling them how they're going to benefit when they work with you instead of what they're going to save. **Most people are willing to pay a little more if they feel more comfortable or trust they're going to get the best bang for their buck.**

And this doesn't mean the cheapest or least expensive. This means how much value are they going to receive for their hard earned cash?

If your marketing materials don't communicate value and only focus on numbers, you're missing the boat - and so is your potential client. Also, remember not to focus on just the product or service. It's that dang radio station again... WII FM. People want to hear benefits and how things are going to change their business, life, and more. They want to know that what you're offering is going to make an immediate impact on their bottom line. Focusing on the features of a product won't do that.

Take a look at the iPhone 5. It has a 4 inch screen with 326 ppi and a resolution of 1136 x 640, stereo speakers, the Lightening connector, an A6 processor with 4G LTE access. Pretty cool huh. Did you get all that? Did it make you want to buy the iPhone 5?

Unless you're a tech geek (which is possible), just listing features of the iPhone 5 didn't do too much or even tell you too much. Instead, focus on the benefits such as saying the 4 inch screen welcomes in much needed viewing real estate which allows you to see and experience more on the phone. The screen resolution allows viewing of high definition videos that pop off the screen and create a true viewing experience which other phones lack. The Lightening connector is just that lightening – decreasing the time spent transferring your files and saving you time and energy. The new A6 processor with 4G LTE allows the phone to operate on the fastest networks in the world creating an unparalleled user experience in today's age of multimedia, social networks, and online access.

I could go into much more details about the benefits of the iPhone 5 and can you tell the difference between talking about products and features versus benefits and how it can affect someone's life or business?

Remember, at the heart of a great lead gen and marketing campaign is having a riveting headline that catches a prospects eye. One of the main reasons emails don't get opened or flyers don't get read is because of a lack of a strong headline which entices the person to read it. The person glancing at the title, headline, or subject fails to see anything of interest to them.

23 DIG DEEPER

Since offers are so important, let's take a deeper dive into this topic. First and foremost, make sure you read Mark Joyner's book called what else... "The Irresistible Offer". It has some great information which can make a huge impact in your marketing campaigns.

When writing marketing materials, make sure you finish with a strong statement which identifies the next step in the sales process. For example, instead of saying, "Looking forward to working with you", say, "Looking forward to discussing how we can use social media to increase your business lead generation results by 20% - 30% or more."

Notice that it's specific and spells out a benefit to their business. As they are flooded with people clambering for their time throughout the day, why should they spend time with you instead of someone else? Specify how meeting with you will help or benefit their business and how not talking to you would be detrimental to their business.

24 OFFER, OFFER, OFFER

There are three types of offers that you should be aware of and use in your marketing materials.

The first type is the hard offer or hard sell. While many people don't like using the hard sell, it works. And it works quite well when used at the right time. A hard offer might be one that contains a deadline or creates scarcity. For example, "Call before the end of the month for our 30% special", or "There's only 10 spots left, so call now and lock in your spot!"

This type of offer is used when you want your prospect to take immediate action and want to buy right now. Used at the appropriate time in the sales process, it can be extremely effective for people who are on the fence or are ready to buy right away.

The second type of offer is the soft offer. This kind of offer is one that helps you identify the interest level of your prospect. It does not, however, ask for an immediate purchase or sale from them. This type of offer is typically seen on opt-in pages, "Enter your name and email below to receive your free report today."

The soft offer is used to generate more leads and start the sales process while the hard offer is used to generate more sales near the end of the sales process. Using the soft offer is important to filter out uninterested individuals who will just end up wasting your time.

The third and final type of offer is the Non-offer. What? When is an offer not an offer? When it's a non-offer of course. Seriously. This is when you're not really making an offer, you're just asking for more information because you've identified that the person is not ready to buy at this time.

You might for example use this on a survey or reply card that says, "I'm not interested right now. Please get back to me on ___[DATE]_____", where the prospect fills out the date. Or it could just ask something like, "I'm not interested right now because _____". Where the individual tells you why they're not interested right now.

This information is important for two reasons.

The first reason is for you to do what we call "Play with resistance." Many times if you know why they're not interested, it's really because they are resisting something. If you can find the source of their resistance, then you can show them how your product or service overcomes their challenge and turn them into a buyer.

BEWARE though that this is a more advanced technique and should only be used to benefit the individual or prospect, not just to sell them something they don't need. **"A buyer convinced against their will is of the same opinion still."**

When done improperly, the buyer will have buyer's remorse and worse, be upset that you convinced them to do something they didn't want to do. When done properly, they'll thank you for getting them to the next level and helping them overcome their resistance.

Only use this strategy when you have enough information about the prospect and you know you are helping them overcome their resistance and challenges.

The second reason to use this kind of non-offer is to be able to clean and segment your list. Simply having this information allows you to properly manage your leads and organize when or if you should contact someone at a later time.

In addition, their answers may surprise you and help you modify your marketing materials. There are numerous reasons why someone would not purchase or work with you and you'll never know all the reasons. You'll get a good idea of most of them if you just simply ask though.

Make sure you use these three types of offers at the right time for the right reasons and your sales and opt-in rates will increase for sure.

25 GIVE BIRTH MORE

I just finished talking about the different kinds of offers, testing, and segmenting your customer list. This is something that is not done as often as it should be with businesses and of course a huge mistake on their part. Using a proper CRM or Customer Relationship Management software is key to your success. It will also help you with this next huge mistake businesses make which is spending too much time with prospects that will never buy.

There's a saying out there that says, **"It's easier to give birth than raise a dead horse"**. In other words, it's easier to find a new prospect than it is to continually work with someone who will never buy from you regardless of what you're offering.

There are a couple of reasons why this occurs.

First is that your lead generation strategies don't really filter your clients well enough. Any good lead generation strategy funnels your prospects and qualifies them through a series of messages.

You should only be spending time with "qualified" leads and let your systems do the rest. This way you can be sure that you're spending your valuable time with the right people and not tire-kickers.

In addition, it's o.k. to say NO to a potential client. While most people are always looking for a YES, sometimes saying NO to the wrong clients can be a life saver. This again all depends upon qualifying the lead and making sure you're working with the right people. You'll also discover that sometimes when you say NO to someone that it makes them rethink their position and will convince them to say YES to you.

A good sales funnel combined with a specific lead generation strategy will greatly reduce working with the wrong people and wasting your time. Focus on the people who are ready to buy and who want to work with you and not only will your perception of sales change, you'll also be able to focus on what you love to do and your business will continue to grow and prosper.

26 BE A LEAD GEN SAMURAI

Back in the day, the Samurai were considered military nobility. The constantly strove for Kaizen or Continuous Improvement and ritually followed a set of rules. In this book, you've been shown a set of rules for lead generation. If you want to succeed in lead generation, it's important for you to follow these rules and avoid the mistakes that I've shared.

When done properly, lead generation can generate buckets of clients and customers who are happy, educated, and most importantly, ready to purchase from you. Follow these fundamentals and rules and avoid the mistakes and you're lead generation strategies will become your lifeline.

In closing though, I want to emphasize the importance of two things.

First, **you must have a proper lead generation, sales, and marketing strategy.** It's useless to generation thousands of leads if you don't have the systems in place in order to handle those leads and convert them into paying clients. You have to have the proper follow-up systems in place to help you build rapport with your leads and filter out the time wasters.

Sit down and write down your different sales funnels as part of an overall marketing strategy and be laser focused on results. Test things to see what works and what doesn't and automate as much as possible. Lead generation can be all consuming when done improperly and extremely exciting and rewarding when done properly.

The second bit of advice I want to close out with is that **marketing is a learned skill and art which every business owner needs to understand including you**. There's simply no replacement for good marketing skills. Writing powerful headlines, sub-headlines, and marketing pieces are critical to your business's success. That's why good copywriters are extremely expensive and can cost upwards of $10,000 - $20,000 for a single page of content.

A good piece of marketing material may still generate leads even if the marketing strategy is poor or non-existent.

Here's a short list of recommend reading to help you improve on your marketing acumen:

- Million Dollar Mailings by Denison Hatch
- Hypnotic Writing: How to Seduce and Persuade Customers with Only Your Words by Joe Vitale
- The Ultimate Sales Letter: Attract New Customers. Boost your Sales by Dan S. Kennedy
- Tribes: We Need You to Lead Us by Seth Godin
- Purple Cow, New Edition: Transform Your Business by Being Remarkable by Seth Godin

Master the art of marketing and follow the rules of lead generation and you'll soon become a lead gen samurai!

APPENDIX: MASSIVE TRAFFIC STRATEGIES

This book focuses on the fundamentals of Lead Generation, and on the mistakes that most businesses make in professional lead generation and how you can avoid them. I wanted to throw in a short and quick summary of the many different lead generation strategies out there though so you can be well on your way to generating multiple streams of leads. Please note that this is a summary and not a complete guide to traffic. That would take several more books to cover, so please just use this as a starting point to look into some very effective methods to generating traffic.

Your Traffic Plan

Before we get into the different strategies and techniques, the first thing you need to do is sit down and ask yourself a few questions.

Here are my top 3 questions to ask.

1) How Much Time Will It Take To Implement These Methods
2) How Much Money Do I Have In My Budget For Traffic
3) How Much Time Can I Devote To Traffic Generation Each Day
   a. What Are The Top Three Free Traffic Methods You Want To Use First
   b. What Is The One Paid Traffic Method You Want To Use First

I know, I said 3 questions only the last question was broken up into a few parts.

First, you need to know that every strategy is different and will require a certain amount of time to implement. Strategies like PPC while may seem quick, actually require more time to be effective as there's a learning curve associated to it. Placing a free ad on Craigslist can also be fairly quick and easy and that too has a learning curve if you want to do it properly. So make sure you allocate the proper amount of time per technique and put together a strategy for implementation.

It's also important to understand the difference between free and paid advertising. While you should get away with all the free advertising methods you can, there's value in paying for certain methods - especially when you know what you're doing. If you're going to use paid methods, start off small, test to see what works, and then add more money to it. Too often, people spend a lot of money upfront when they don't know what they're doing and then get discouraged. Don't let this be you. Test, test, test! And make sure you track your results as well.

Once you answer those three (or five) questions, then you should decide when you're going to start and then take MASSIVE Action to implement those strategies and watch your results!

So without further adieu, let's jump right into it.

1) Pay Per Click Advertising

Pay Per Click Advertising is often referred to as performance-based advertising. In other words, you pay for your results, not for the exposure.

For example, when you advertise in the newspaper, you get an ad on a page somewhere only that doesn't guarantee that anyone goes to your website or business.

With PPC Advertising, you only pay when someone "Clicks" on your link. Your ad can be shown 1000 times and you still won't pay unless someone clicks on your ad and goes to your site. This is a great way of getting traffic if you know what you're doing.

Tips

i. The Headline Is The Most Important Part of PPC. Choosing the right headline can be the difference between making sales and losing a lot of money. Make sure you have a headline which grabs the user's attention. Make sure it's something that you yourself would want to read.

ii. Split Testing Is Critical
1. You have to test your ads to see which one works the best. This again can be a life saver - or a money saver.
2. Split Testing involves placing two identical ads where only one word or phrase is changed to see which one performs better. Keep the one that performs better and split-test it again. Change another word and test. Then do it again. Keep testing until you have an ad that converts well.

3. As with all testing, make sure you're tracking your results. It's important to see what ad is working and which one is not. If you don't then you may change the wrong one.

4. Use a sample size which is enough to get results only large enough to not be a fluke. You don't want to just test with 10 people. That's not enough to tell you if something works or not. You need a couple hundred impressions before you can actually see results. The best thing to do is set a budget for all your tests and then see how many impressions you can get within that budget. Depending upon the keywords you're using some budgets may be higher than others. Don't spend too much money here though as you want to save your money for a larger campaign after you're done testing.

iii. Limited Space (Typically 25 Characters)

1. PPC Campaign ads typically only give you 25 characters or less to get your message across. Choose your words carefully and be succinct. Make sure you throw in a call to action and a website. Use named, key-word hyperlinks instead of the actual URL to save space. For example, use "Dog Training" with a hyperlink instead of directly using http://www.mydogtrainingwebsite.com which can take up more space.

iv. Emphasize Your Offer On The Opt-In Page And Not The Product Itself

1. Many people fail to do this and end up spending a lot of money unnecessarily! Drive traffic to an Opt-in Page, not a product or service page. Get their information and then market to them via an email campaign.

2.   This is extremely important as almost all people on the internet first get on to find information, not to purchase something.   So offer them a good piece of information, something enticing, something that will make them want to come back for more. Make it unique if possible and make sure you have a fantastic headline!

Sites

You may have heard of some of the bigger sites like Google Adwords only there are several smaller websites which are less expensive and can still get you good traffic. Here's a list of some of them for you to look at:

1. www.Adwords.google.com
2. www.searchmarketing.yahoo.com
3. www.miva.com/US/content/advertiser/pay_per_click. asp
4. www.adcenter.microsoft.com
5. www.enhance.com
6. www.goclick.com
7. www.7search.com

2) Classifieds Adverting Campaigns

When someone hears classified ads, they most likely think of print ads. Print ads in major publications can cost an arm and a leg and not get very good results when done improperly.

The growth of the internet though has created an entirely new marketing medium for classified ads - namingly, online classified ads. Online classified ads a wonderful because many of them are free or very inexpensive and it helps market your opportunity, product, or service to millions of people instead of just thousands in your area.

Here are some guidelines and tips when using online classified ads:

a. Headline Is The Most Important. Use a good eye-catching headline to attract readers.
b. Split Test - Again, I cannot stress the importance of this.
c. There are many free and paid advertising sites. Start off with the free ones listed below. The paid ones are usually authority or highly ranked sites and can be quite expensive.
d. Sites
   i. Www.Craigslist.Org
   ii. Www.Usfreeads.Com
   iii. Www.Adpost.Com

3) Banner / Text-Link Advertising

a. These are Specific Sites With Advertising Opportunities
   i. These sites are where the owner has a blurb about how they are willing to advertise your ad on their website. You need to contact them directly to see what they will charge you to do this.
   ii. This strategy is good with very specific niche websites and may cost you some money.
b. Ad Networks
   i. Ad Networks Allow Site Owners To Have A Steady Stream Of Different Advertisers Running Ads On Their Sites Without Having To Deal Directly With Those Advertisers.

    ii. Site Owners Join The Network, Specify Requirements, And Then Past Some Code Into Their Web Pages That Will Rotate Ads On Autopilot.

    iii. Sites

        1. Www.Ad-Venture.Com

        2. Www.Adace.Com

        3. Google Adsense

4) Press Releases

Press releases are the number one advertising medium of the media for the past 50 years and continues to produce great results.

Press releases are easy to use and should be done before and after you hold events or make announcements. With online press releases, you can use them for basically anything new with your company including new product or service releases, awards given and received, events, and more.

Here are some quick press release tips.

    a. Short-Term Boost However, a well-written, key-word-rich press release can rank very high in the search engines and bring you a steady stream of traffic over the long term.

    b. Must Be A Newsworthy Event

    c. Must Follow A Specific Format

    d. www.PRWeb.com is the granddaddy of Press Release sites

5) E-Zine Advertising

E-Zine is short for Electronic Magazine. Advertising on popular e-zines is a great way to get huge exposure for your business. Look for e-zines within your niche to increase your conversion rates.

Here are some additional tips:

a. Short Term Traffic
b. Google Your Niche Keyword Plus "E-Zine" Or "Newsletter"
c. Tips
   i. Use An Effective Headline
   ii. Track Your Advertisements (Monster Response Account)
   iii. Start Small And Micro-Test
   iv. Keep An Eye On Branding
   v. Repetition
   vi. Use Tested And Proven Copy.
   vii. Consult With The Publisher If Possible
   viii. Drive People To Your Opt-In Page.
d. Sites
   i. Www.Ezineadvertising.Com
   ii. Www.Onlineforsuccess.Com/Ezine-Marketing-Directory.Htm
   iii. Www.Ezine-Dir.Com

6) Article Marketing

Article marketing entails the writing of an article on a particular niche or topic. Once you have a informational and value packed article, then you would blast that article to numerous article marketing sites. People from all parts of the world go to article marketing sites to find information on their particular search and if your article is written well enough, your article will pop up in their search.

There is no marketing information in the article you write though. Instead, if a person is interested in you or more information about your article, your information along with a link to your website is placed inside your signature box. They will simply click on your signature box and go to your website.

Article marketing is an excellent way to generate huge traffic for your site. Here are some quick tips about article marketing:

a. Why
   i. Longer Term Traffic As Your Articles Stay Out On The Internet Indefinitely
   ii. Provide Useful Information
   iii. Key Word Rich
   iv. Build Credibility

b. Questions To Ask
 i. Would I Learn Something New By Reading This
 ii. Would I Enjoy The Author's Style Of Conveying Information
 iii. Would I Trust What The Author Is Telling Me
 iv. Would I Want To Read More Of The Author's Work

c. Articles should be keyword rich and 300 - 500 words

d. Submission Sites
 i. Www.Articlecity.Com
 ii. Www.Ezinearticles.Com
 iii. Www.Ezine-Dir.Com

7) Marketing Forums / Groups

Forums continue to be a great way to share information between users. Here's how to use them to your advantage to drive huge amounts of traffic.

a. Find Forums Or Groups Pertaining To Your Market Or Niche

b. Make Sure They Get Traffic On A Regular Basis

c. Register An Account And Start Reading To Get A Feel Of The Community

d. Introduce Yourself And Participate

e. Place A Short Advertisement With A Link To Your Opt-In Page In Your Signature File

8) Stealing Traffic From Blogs

Blogs are a great way to get traffic. This doesn't mean you have to have your own award winning blog though. Here's a quick method to get tons of traffic from other people's blogs.

a. Join blogs as a commenter and create a signature file with your website in it.
b. Post Responses Or Comments On Popular Blogs
    i. People will see your comments and if they like you, they will look you up or go to your website which is listed in your signature file.
c. Search Through Blog Directories
    i. Www.Blogcatalog.Com
    ii. Dir.Blogflux.Com
    iii. Blogsearchengine.Com

9) Stealing More Traffic From Big-Name Sites

As with stealing traffic from blogs, this isn't really stealing. You're in essence riding the wave of an authority site or a popular site. By posting comments, answering questions, and providing value on different sites and blogs, people will view you as an expert and go to your website.

a. Sites
b. Www.Amazon.Com
c. Epinions.Com
d. Ask.Metafilter.Com

10) Social Networking

Social networking continues to grow with over 250,000 social networks out there. Used properly, social networks are an incredible source of lead generation.

    a. Squidoo - Allows you to create webpages without knowing HTML and you can put links back to your website.

    b. Hubpages - Allows you to create webpages without knowing HTML and you can put links back to your website. Competes with Squidoo, only you should use both!

    c. Facebook - Over 1 Billion users says you should be on this network! The potential traffic is huge!

    d. LinkedIn and Twitter are also must join networks and so is fast growing Google Plus.

11) Viral Video And Podcasting

Cisco and Yahoo estimate that by 2013, 90% of all internet traffic will be video. Video continues to grow and become more prevalent in our society. If you're not using video to generate leads, you're missing the boat. Love it or leave it, it's a must have if you want to grow your internet presence and generate more leads online.

a. Make funny videos and they'll go viral when people see them. Make boring videos and only 3 people will see them (You, Your Significant Other, and Your Mom)

b. Video
   i. Youtube
   ii. Google Video
   iii. Revver

c. Podcasting
   i. Podcast.Net
   ii. Apple Itunes
   iii. Podcast Blaster

12) Content Syndication And Setting Up Your Own Blog

Blogs have been popular since 1998 and continue to grow. People just like to read about other people. Having your own blog helps establish your credibility and authority. Using RSS or Really Simple Syndication helps you get the word out about your blog. Here are some sites to be aware of when you have your own blog:

- a. Submit Your Articles To Rss Syndication Sites
  - i. RSS Stands for Really Simple Syndication
  - ii. Www.Goarticles.Com
  - iii. Www.Freesticky.Com
  - iv. Www.Freewebsubmission.Com
- b. Blogging Resources
  - i. Www.Blogger.Com
  - ii. Www.Wordpress.Com
  - iii. Netforbeginners.About.Com/Od/Bloggingbasics

13) Viral Reports

Viral reports are just that. Reports that become viral. These are quick, simply, and easy to create and can be spread throughout the internet. They don't have to be very long and can create tremendous amounts of traffic for your website.

- a. Create Your Own Reports
    - i. Provide Quality Content
    - ii. Give It Away For Free
    - iii. Allow Distributors To Rebrand It With Their Affiliate Links
- b. www.Viralpdf.Com Allows You To Make All Or Part Of The Affiliate Links In Your Report Rebrandable.
- c. Ebook Distribution Sites
    - i. Www.Mindlikewater.Com
    - ii. Www.Ebookpalace.Com
    - iii. Www.Jogena.Com

14) **Natural Search Engine Optimization**

There's really no substitute for natural SEO or Search Engine Optimization. All the search engines use their own "algorithm" to determine which results come up top when someone types in a word in their search engine. By making it easier for search engines to find your content, you're more likely to come up top.

Natural SEO takes time and patience and when done properly, generates huge, long-lasting results. Focus on adding regular content to your website or blog and over time, you'll get ranked naturally.

Here are some more tips to help you get those higher rankings:

    a. Know Your Key Word Phrases
        i. Tool.Motoricera.Info/Keyword-Density
        ii. Should Carry A Keyword Density Of 12 - 15 Percent
    b. Have The Key Word Phrase In Your Title Tag
    c. Use The Key Phrase In The Body Title Of Your Web Page <H2> Tag
    d. Key Phrase Should Appear Within Bold Tag At Least Once
    e. Use Your Key Phrase Multiple Times Within Your Copy - Make It Sound Natural
        i. Use LSI Keywords
    f. Include Key Phrases In Named Hyperlinks
    g. Use Alt Tag With Your Images

15) List Building And Email Campaigns

All Traffic should be driven to somewhere with an Opt-In form where you can build a list and create an email campaign in order to market to people over and over and over again - at least until they unsubscribe or buy! In order for this to succeed, you need four things.

    a. Website With Your Own Domain, You'll Have...
        i. More Control over the presentation of Marketing materials and product offerings
        ii. Dedicated lead generation
        iii. Branding and visibility
        iv. control over the flow of web site traffic
        v. ability to interact with and respond to visitors
    b. Autoresponder Service is a Must! I use and recommend Trafficwave.
        i. http://bit.ly/TrafficWaveAutoresponder
    c. Link-Tracking Software - You have to know where your traffic is coming from
    d. Link-Cloaking Software - Mask long, ugly links using link-Cloaking software . I recommend www.Bit.Ly

That's it for now. Use this information wisely and constantly refine your lead gen strategies to become your own lead gen samurai!

ABOUT THE AUTHOR

Chaffee-Thanh Nguyen is an Entrepreneur, Success Coach, Shining Son, Loving Brother, Faithful Husband, Doting Father, Playful Uncle, and Fun and Dependable Friend (with a bit of Crazy). He is the founder of Key Concept Coaching and has traveled the country working with small business owners and entrepreneurs to SYSTEMize their business, control their finances, develop their brand, increase their marketing exposure, and master their minds.

Combining his experience working in a Fortune 500 company as an Engineer, Certified Project Manager with PMI, Senior IT Business Analyst and his background in public speaking, subconscious reprogramming, and mindset mastery, he has been able to help thousands of individuals across the country through his public speaking, event coaching, and personal mentoring. He has a strong commitment to helping others achieve their hidden potential. He also runs the Chicago Entrepreneur Meetup Group, is a Certified National Trainer with JCI (Junior Chamber International), and an Illinois JCI Senator.

Printed in Great Britain
by Amazon